THE ESSENCE OF SPIRITUAL DISCIPLINE

Principles of Successful Discipleship

Deborah Sheppard

COPYRIGHT 2018 Deborah Sheppard

THE ESSENCE OF SPIRITUAL DISCIPLINE

All Rights Reserved

Scriptures marked KJV are taken from the KING JAMES VERSION (KJV): KING JAMES VERSION, public domain.

Scripture quotations marked (NLT) are taken from the Holy Bible, New Living Translation, copyright ©1996, 2004, 2007, 2013, 2015 by Tyndale House Foundation. Used by permission of Tyndale House Publishers, Inc., Carol Stream, Illinois 60188. All rights reserved.

Scripture quotations marked (NIV) are taken from the Holy Bible, New International Version®, NIV®. Copyright © 1973, 1978, 1984, 2011 by Biblica, Inc.TM Used by permission of Zondervan. All rights reserved worldwide. www.zondervan.com The "NIV" and "New International Version" are trademarks registered in the United States Patent and Trademark Office by Biblica, Inc.TM

Scripture quotations taken from the Amplified® Bible (AMPC),
Copyright © 1954, 1958, 1962, 1964, 1965, 1987 by The Lockman Foundation Used by permission. www.Lockman.org

Scripture quotations marked (AMP) are taken from the Amplified Bible, Copyright © 1954, 1958, 1962, 1964, 1965, 1987 by The Lockman Foundation. Used by permission.

Scripture quotations marked MSG are taken from *THE MESSAGE*, copyright © 1993, 1994, 1995, 1996, 2000, 2001, 2002 by Eugene H. Peterson. Used by permission of NavPress. All rights reserved. Represented by Tyndale House Publishers, Inc.

Scripture quotations are from the ESV® Bible (The Holy Bible, English Standard Version®), copyright © 2001 by Crossway, a publishing ministry of Good News Publishers. Used by permission. All rights reserved.

This book may not be reproduced, transmitted or stored in whole or in part by any means, including graphic, electronic or mechanical without the express written consent of the publisher except in case of brief quotations embodied in critical articles and reviews.

ISBN: 978-0-9997159-4-9

ALPHA BOOK PUBLISHING

4132 E. Joppa Rd. Suite 1123

Notthingham MD, 21236

TABLE OF CONTENTS

	Introduction	1
I.	Preparation Sessions	4
II.	*Week One* — Challenge Session	12
III.	*Week Two* — Learn	20
IV.	*Week Three* — Embrace	32
V.	*Week Four* — Defensive Fighting Techniques	41
VI.	*Week Five* — Strategic Session	52
VII.	*Week Six* — Final Evaluation	65
VIII.	Accomplishments	72

DEDICATION

This manual is dedicated to Believers who are in pursuit of a goal in Christ Jesus. There's always a believer who wants it ALL. Spiritual Discipline requires you to push yourself harder and further than you ever thought possible. With prayer, meditation, fasting, proper diet, and exercise, your mind, body, soul, and spirit must be fit to achieve the ultimate goals. It's vital that you prepare not only for your training, but also your transition into victorious faith as a walking Believer. If you seek to get more out of life, this book is dedicated to you. Challenge yourself to go higher! Let's Go! Now! Your journey officially begins. The Holy Spirit will guide you through your transformation during the next six weeks.

Spiritually Submitted,
Apostle Deborah Sheppard

SPECIAL THANKS

With all my love to my amazing husband, Apostle Wayne Sheppard, my mother, Aurena Hunt, my prayer warrior, Prophetess Marika, Linda, and the Unveiling Church Family, for pushing me to pursue my full purpose.

To my three sons, Immanuel, Duke, and Elijah for your love. Finally, Counselor Tamara Woods, you are so amazing; you jumped in and helped me to birth this book. I am forever grateful!

God bless you ALL!

INTRODUCTION

This study was based on a personal walk with God, and walking with other believers. One would think following Christ is the beginning of no problems, when in actuality it is beginning the walk of Faith. One would have to come to the knowledge of trusting God for everything. Being a believer officially begins with *The Essence of Spiritual Discipline*. It is a challenging experience both physically and mentally, but will transform you ultimately from spiritual immaturity (drinking milk) to spiritual maturity (eating strong meat).

The Bible declares, according to 1 Corinthians 3:2 (NIV), *I gave you milk, not solid food, for you were not yet ready for solid food. In fact, you are still not ready.*

Most believers do not study to learn how to walk with God, they just follow a customary pattern as church-goers. To be a successful believer in Christ, one must study the Word of God to learn how to grow from an immature believer to a mature believer. One thing must be understood; a typical follower of Christ must become a CONFIDENT BELIEVER. The Word of God will give the believer skills to achieve the needed confidence to excel as a SOUND faith walker of Christ.

The Bible declares, according to Ephesians 6:5-18 (ESV),

Servants, be obedient to them that are your masters according to the flesh, with fear and trembling, in singleness of your heart, as unto Christ; 6 Not with eye service, as men pleasers; but as the servants of Christ, doing the will of God from the heart; 7 With good will do service, as to the Lord, and not to men: 8 Knowing that whatsoever good thing any man doeth, the same shall he receives of the Lord, whether he be bond or free. 9 And, ye masters, do the same things unto them, forbearing threatening: knowing that your Master also is in heaven; neither is there respect of persons with him. 10 Finally, my brethren, be strong in the Lord, and in the power of his might. 11 Put on the whole Armour of God, that ye may be able to stand against the wiles of the devil. 12 For we wrestle not against flesh and blood, but against principalities, against powers, against the rulers of the darkness of this world, against spiritual wickedness in high places. 13 Wherefore take unto you the whole armour of God, that ye may be able to withstand in the evil day, and having done all, to stand. 14 Stand therefore, having your loins girt about with truth, and having on the breastplate of righteousness; 15 And your feet shod with the preparation of the gospel of peace; 16 Above all, taking the shield of faith, wherewith ye shall be able to quench all the fiery darts of the wicked. 17 And take the helmet of salvation, and the sword of the Spirit, which is the word of God: 18 Praying always with all prayer and supplication in the Spirit, and watching thereunto with all perseverance and supplication for all saints;

Remember, *The Essence of Spiritual Discipline* teaches the believer how to solely TRUST GOD. One can't just quote Scriptures; the believer must become what he or she quotes!

Let's Pray

Thank you, Jesus, for this excellent opportunity to walk with you. Teach me, oh Lord, how to submit to your authority in your Word, so I can be filled with the knowledge of your will in all wisdom and spiritual understanding; that I might walk worthy of You, Lord, unto all pleasing, being fruitful in every good work, and increasing in the knowledge of God; strengthened with all might, according to your glorious power, unto all patience and longsuffering with joyfulness; giving thanks unto the Father, which hath made me meet to be partakers of the inheritance of the saints in light: who hath delivered me from the power of darkness, and hath translated me into the Kingdom of His dear Son: in whom I have redemption through His blood, even the forgiveness of sins, (KJV Colossian 1:9-14) in Jesus Christ's name. Amen!

PREPARATION SESSIONS

By accepting Jesus Christ as our Lord and Savior, we are also taking the responsibility of becoming soldiers for the Kingdom of God. Matthew 28:19 says, "*Go therefore and make disciples of all the nations, baptizing them in the name of the Father and the Son and the Holy Spirit.*" In exchange for the salvation of our souls from sins, Satan, and the thralls of Hell, we are willingly and cheerfully giving our service to the Kingdom of God. That is a reasonable and acceptable service to God. No soldier in any army is expected to fight or defend a cause without proper training. This philosophy is no less critical to the Army of Believers.

God is ready to shower you with everything that you need to be successful in this 6-week Spiritual Basic Training. If you are seeking to enlist in the Armed Forces of the United States of America, there is a period that you must successfully master, and that is called "Basic Training." You are not required at enlistment to be omniscient of the tactics of the enemy nor your regiment's techniques. 2 Corinthians 3:5 AMPC reminds us "*not that we are fit (qualified and sufficient inability) of ourselves to perform, but our power and ability and sufficiency are from God."* This study qualifies those that have answered the call for service. The main component in this boot camp is denying yourself and yielding to the will of our Father.

Take Up Your Cross and Follow Jesus

Luke 9:23-27 MSG, then he told them what they could expect for themselves: *"Anyone who intends to come with me has to let me lead. You're not in the driver's seat—I am. Don't run from suffering; embrace it. Follow me and I'll show you how. Self-help is no help at all. Self-sacrifice is the way, my way, to finding yourself, your true self. What good would it do to get everything you want and lose you, the real you? If any of you is embarrassed with me and the way I'm leading you, know that the Son of Man will be far more embarrassed with you when he arrives in all his splendor in company with the Father and the holy angels. This isn't, you realize, pie in the sky by and by. Some who have taken their stand right here are going to see it happen, see with their own eyes the kingdom of God."*

Note, the Scripture states we are not in the driver's seat, the first thing we must learn to do is allow God to lead and guide us to ALL truths.

In preparation for this spiritual discipline course, you will notice a few reoccurring themes. This preparation is designed to prepare you as well as explain the importance of what you must acquire and maintain as you go through this arduous process.

* Develop an Effective Prayer Life.

James 5:16 (NIV) — *The effectual fervent prayer of a righteous man availeth much.*

Prayer is a communication process that allows us to talk to God. Prayer is the practice of the presence of God. It is the place where pride is abandoned, hope is lifted, and supplication is made. Prayer is the place of admitting our need, of adopting humility, and claiming dependence upon God.

* Stay Motivated.

Romans 12:11(ESV) — *Do not be slothful in zeal, be fervent in spirit, serve the Lord.*

Something motivated you to accept the calling. What was that thing that initially motivated you? Keep that in mind as you go through the next six weeks.

* Recite and Memorize Several Scriptures Daily.

Colossians 3:16 (KJV) — *Let the word of Christ dwell in you richly in all wisdom; teaching, and admonishing one another in psalms and hymns and spiritual songs, singing with grace in your hearts to the Lord.*

Get the strength you need through the Word of God. Read, recite, and implement Scriptures daily.

* Strive for Excellence.

Colossians 3:23 (ESV) — *Whatever you do, work heartily, as for the Lord and not for men.*

When you are working on a skill, do your very best to give your best. This is a personal journey, and your goal is to grow. Do not do just enough, push yourself to the next day you are in a better place.

* Build Your Endurance.

1 Thessalonians (NIV) 5:17-18 — *Pray continually, give thanks*

in all circumstances; for this is God's will for you.

When things get tough, and they will, do not give up. Finding time, energy, and the exact words will be challenging in this process. Endure and push through these barriers and do not give up.

* Assemble with Others.

Hebrews 10:25 (AMP) — *Not forsaking {or} neglecting to assemble [as believers], as is the habit of some people, but admonishing (warning, urging, and encouraging).*

This is not the time to isolate yourself. Have a reliable support system, participate in worship service, and share your experiences, good and bad, in this process.

* Be Teachable and Open to the Voice of God.

Proverbs 12:1 The Message (MSG) — *If you love learning, you love the discipline that goes with it—how shortsighted to refuse correction!*

Each week, you will be able to build on the skills from the previous week so you can grow during this training.

This is not an easy journey, but it is indeed well worth the ride.

Notes

Notes

Notes

Notes

~ *Week One* ~

CHALLENGE SESSION

This week, God is challenging you both mentally and physically. You will learn the necessary steps of a believer's life and also condition your body for the physical requirements to become an adequate faith walker.

Your daily sessions should always start with prayer, meditation, and listening to the voice of God. We have to be able to discern the voice of God. The Bible declares in Hebrew 4:12 (ESV), *For the word of God is living and active, sharper than any two-edged sword, piercing to the division of soul and of spirit, of joints and morrow, and discerning the thoughts and intentions of the heart.*

Let's Pray

Today is a new day, and I pray that you fill me up, God, with Wisdom, Knowledge, and Understanding, so I will not only be a Bible quote-er, but will live it; with the Holy Spirit as my guide. My spiritual senses are open to smell your fragrance, and hear your heart beating inside of my soul. Amen.

This will be a week of you starting fresh; both mentally and physically. Your challenge will be to kick out those old thoughts and replace them with godly new ones, according to Isaiah 43:18-19 (ESV), *"Remember not the former things, nor consider the things of old. Behold, I am doing a new thing; now it springs forth, do you not perceive it? I will make a way in the wilderness and rivers in the desert."* Open your heart and mind and allow God to reside in you.

Learn and practice the basic steps of a believer in life and condition your body for the physical requirements needed to become an adequate faith-walking believer.

In this first session, your study time should be dedicated to the Word and studying *you*. You need to know who you are, the true you! Be more aware of your reactions and mood changes this week. Make a concerted effort in writing down the situations God brings to your attention. Then write what you are saying to yourself or others during those elevated or sunken moments. 2 Corinthians 10:5 (KJV) encourages believers to *"cast down imaginations, and every high thing that exalteth itself against the knowledge of God, and bringing into captivity every thought to the obedience of Christ."* Work on replacing those reactions or thoughts with the thoughts and reactions of God.

The first week, start to build a Scripture-based prayer life. The Bible declares we are overcomers by the Blood of the Lamb and the words of our testimony. We are building our faith with the Word of God so that we can have new and powerful testimonies. God's Word has to be the focus when we pray and meditate. This is the time to get *up and close* to the Word. The Book of Psalms is good for this week. In this book of the Bible, you can find prayers, songs, and stories for every situation you deal with. This is a good time to learn and understand that the Word of God is the weapon that will defeat the wiles of the enemy and our own voice (2 Corinthians 10:3-6 The Message, MSG).

The world is unprincipled. It's dog-eat-dog out there! The world doesn't fight fair. But we don't live or fight our battles that way—never have and never will. The tools of our trade aren't for marketing or manipulation, but they are for demolishing that entire massively corrupt culture. We use our powerful God-tools for smashing warped philosophies, tearing down barriers erected against the Truth of God, and fitting every loose thought and emotion and impulse into the structure of life shaped by Christ. Our tools are ready at hand for clearing the ground of every obstruction and building lives of obedience into maturity.

Reminders for the Week:

* Read the Word at Least One Hour Per Day.

This can be broken down throughout the day or in one setting. Make this time intimate and purposeful.

* Practice Getting in the Presence of God in an Intimate Way.

Learn what is best for you. It may be listening to music, doing chores, driving, walking, etc. God doesn't forbid being creative with this intimate time. This is your time to discover you.

* Exercise Spiritually and Physically.

Practice declarations and prayers from Psalms and become more aware of the nutrition that your body needs. Drink water; substitute unhealthy food selections for healthier ones.

Notes

Notes

Notes

Notes

LEARN

This week, God is challenging you to learn and integrate the walk and language of Christ in your life. You will become aware of the *spiritual doors* that are gateways into your spirit.

Your daily sessions should always start with prayer, meditation, and listening to the voice of God. As you study the life of Christ this week, remember that you are to enjoy and ingest the accounts of the writers of the Gospels. But also in meditation, be open to what God wants you to learn from the accounts that you read. Proverbs 4:7 (KJV) reminds us — *in all our getting, get understanding.*

Let's Pray

Lord Jesus, this is a personal walk with you that has become NECESSARY! I will take control over my life by your power and the authority you have given unto me. Lord, you sent your Word to me to heal me and to deliver me from destruction. Amen.

God will teach you through His Word the life of Christ, and His obedience to God (Jesus said I do nothing of myself, only what God tells me). Begin preparing for your role as a Child of the Most-High God! By Faith!

This second week of studying, read the accounts of Jesus that were written by Mark, Matthew, Luke, and John. 1 Corinthians 2:9-13(KJV) states, *"But as it is written, Eye hath not seen, nor ear heard, neither have entered into the heart of man, the things which God hath prepared for them that love him. But God hath revealed them unto us by his Spirit... Now we have received, not the spirit of the world, but the spirit which is of God; that we might know the things that are freely given to us of God. Which things also we speak, not in the words which man's wisdom teacheth, but which the Holy Ghost teacheth; comparing spiritual things with spiritual."*

Dedicate at least one hour per day to reading and studying the Word this week. To build endurance, you may do 15-minute intervals to getting to know Jesus Christ by reading the gospels as though they were autobiographies.

Begin to set goals this week, Write these goals down. The Bible reads in Habakkuk 2:2 (KJV), *And the Lord answered me: "Write the vision; make it plain on tablets, so he may run who reads it.* At the beginning of the week, make a broad goal that you are planning to accomplish. This is a simple goal that is plausible in a short period—this week. This is a goal that is personal to you, one that you are willing to and able to accomplish. In creating this goal, think about resources that you have at your disposal. After you have decided and written down your goal, write smaller goals for each day that lead to accomplishing your goal of the week. Monitor your progress often and do not get dissuaded if you find yourself adjusting your smaller goals.

In your meditation time, trust that God desires to teach you and be intimate with you. Genesis 3:9 records God's desire to be close to us, *Then the LORD God called to the man, and said to him, "Where are you?"* There are many scriptural accounts of God calling out and desiring to be intimate with His people. Here are some examples: Abraham (Genesis 22:11), Jacob (Genesis 46: 1-4), Moses (Exodus 3:1), Samuel (1 Samuel 3:1), Martha (Luke10: 38), and Simon (Luke 22:31). You are no different; He is calling your name. Listen to hear what He is telling you about your walk with Him, how to best learn from the walk of His Son Jesus Christ, and how He wants you to walk and talk for the Kingdom of God.

In this intimate time, begin by cleansing your mind. This cleansing begins with creating a peaceful environment in a place in which there will be limited interruptions. A place and time that is calming and safe will make this cleansing more helpful. This is exercising your physical being to be under subjection to the Will of God (Romans. 12:2 KJV). Renew your mind at each meditation period, concentrate on your heart breathing and on a Scripture that creates a sense of peace for you. It is important that you have an arsenal of Scriptures so that you have choices, depending on your situation. Practice getting in the presence of God and the stillness of God. As the week comes to an end, this spiritual exercise must become more deliberate and purposeful.

Consecration is a word that you may have heard in many situations. In the field of medicine, you need to consecrate, cleanse your internal organs, and restrict eating or have only certain foods intake to obtain accurate testing results. Certain religions have a period of fasting and consecration to observe traditions and holidays. These fasts can be a sacrificial limitation of activities, adhering to strict eating habits, and increased religious participation. For believers in the Kingdom of God, fasting and consecration should be an intrinsic part of our lives.

Joshua 3:5 — *Then Joshua said to the people, "Consecrate yourselves, for tomorrow the Lord will do wonders among you."*

2 Corinthians 6:17 (MSG) gives more instruction of what a consecrated life should look like *"Don't become partners with those who reject God. How can you make a partnership out of right and wrong? That's not partnership; that's war. Is light best friends with dark? Does Christ go strolling with the Devil? Do trust and mistrust hold hands? Who would think of setting up pagan idols in God's holy Temple? But that is exactly what we are, each of us a temple in whom God lives. God himself put it this way: "I'll live in them, move into them; I'll be their God, and they'll be my people. So leave the corruption and compromise; leave it for good," says God. "Don't link up with those who will pollute you. I want you all for myself. I'll be a Father to you; you'll be sons and daughters to me." The Word of the Master, God."*

Matthew 6:16 (ESV) says, *"And when you fast, do not look gloomy like the hypocrites, for they disfigure their faces that their fasting may be seen by others. Truly, I say to you, they have received their reward."*

Reminders for the Week:

* Learn How to Get in the Presence of God: Study and Recite Worship Scriptures.

David wrote in Psalm 63:1 (KJV), "O God, thou art my God, early will I seek thee. My soul thirsts for Thee, my flesh longs for thee in a dry and thirsty land, where there is no water."

Solomon wrote something similar in Proverbs 8:17 (KJV), "I love them that love me; and those who seek me early shall find me."

James 4:8 (KJV) says, "Draw near to God, and He will draw near to you." We will seek God and find Him when we seek Him with all of our heart (Jeremiah 29:13 NIV).

* Test the Spirits.

1 John 4 English Standard Version (ESV) reads, *4 "Beloved, do not believe every spirit, but test the Spirits to see whether they are from God, for many false prophets have gone out into the world. 2 By this you know the Spirit of God: every spirit that confesses that Jesus Christ has come in the flesh is from God, 3 and every spirit that does not confess Jesus is not from God. This is the spirit of the antichrist, which you heard was coming and now is in the world already.4 Little children, you are from God and have overcome them, for he who is in you is greater than he who is in the world. 5 They are from the world; therefore they speak from the world, and the world listens to them. 6 We are from God. Whoever knows God listens to us; whoever is not from God does not listen to us. By this, we know the Spirit of truth and the spirit of error."*

* Begin to Learn Your Spiritual Weapons.

Ephesian chapter 6 clearly states, 11 "Put on the whole armour of God, that ye may be able to stand against the wiles of the devil. 12 For we wrestle not against flesh and blood, but against principalities, against powers, against the rulers of the darkness of this world, against spiritual wickedness in high places. 13 Wherefore take unto you the whole Armour of God, that ye may be able to withstand in the evil day, and having done all, to stand. 14 Stand therefore, having your loins girt about with truth, and having on the breastplate of righteousness; 15 And your feet shod with the preparation of the gospel of peace; 16 Above all, taking the shield of faith, wherewith ye shall be able to quench all the fiery darts of the wicked. 17 And take the helmet of salvation, and the sword of the Spirit, which is the word of God: 18 Praying always with all prayer and supplication in the Spirit, and watching thereunto with all perseverance and supplication for all saints;"

The apostle Paul instructs Christians to wage war against the sin in themselves (Romans 6: 2-4 NIV):

What shall we say, then? Shall we go on sinning so that grace may increase? 2 By no means! We are those who have died to sin; how can we live in it any longer? 3 Or don't you know that all of us who were baptized into Christ Jesus were baptized into his death? 4 We were therefore buried with him through baptism into death in order that, just as Christ was raised from the dead through the glory of the Father, we too may live a new life.

Paul also warns us to oppose the schemes of the devil

(Ephesians 6:10–18 NIV), "Finally, be strong in The Lord and in his mighty power. 11 Put on the full armor of God, so that you can take your stand against the devil's schemes. 12 For our struggle is not against flesh and blood, but against the rulers, against the authorities, against the powers of this dark world and against the spiritual forces of evil in the heavenly realms."

* Check Your Spiritual Doors.

Mark 3:27 (NIV) — In fact, no one can enter a strong man's house without first tying him up. Then he can plunder the strong man's house.

1 Peter 5:8 (NIV) — Be alert and of sober mind. Your enemy, the devil, prowls around like a roaring lion looking for someone to devour.

Job 1:7 (ESV) — The LORD said to Satan, "From where do you come?" Then Satan answered the LORD and said, "From roaming about on the earth and walking around on it."

Isaiah 59:19 (KJV) — So shall they fear the name of the Lord from the west, and his glory from the rising of the sun. When the enemy shall come in like a flood, the Spirit of the Lord shall lift up a standard against him.

* Study How to Fight with Scriptures.

Ephesians 6:10–12(NIV) says, "Finally, be strong in the Lord and in his mighty power. Put on the full armor of God so that you can take your stand against the devil's schemes. For our struggle is not against flesh and blood, but against the rulers, against the authorities, against the powers of this dark world and against the spiritual forces of evil in the heavenly realms." This text teaches some crucial truths: we can only stand strong in the Lord's power, it is God's armor that protects us, and our battle is ultimately against spiritual forces of evil in the world.

Obviously, this is an intense training schedule, geared toward reinforcing the principles of discipline and teamwork. From here, you'll look forward to moving toward the rifle range to learn some exciting—and very useful skills.

Notes

Notes

Notes

Notes

EMBRACE

This week, God is arming you with the needed weapons and tactics to be an effective disciple.

Your daily sessions should always start with prayer, meditation, and listening to the voice of God. Then move from learning the walk of Christ to embracing the Will of God. Set your goal this week to include physical as well as spiritual.

Let's Pray

Lord, I will take control over my life by your power and the authority that you have given unto me. Lord, you sent your Word to me to heal me and to deliver me from all my destructions. Today, I become accountable for my actions and my ways, in Jesus' mighty Name. Amen.

As you set goals this week, journal your journey. Write down your experiences, struggles, and questions; so that when you gather with other disciples, you can accurately spread hope and receive support.

This third week, you are setting goals to embrace the Word of God and the ways of God. Webster's Dictionary defines embrace as an act of accepting or supporting something willingly or enthusiastically. During your study and meditation time, focus on 1) filling up, 2) getting fit and giving full attention. As you set goals this week, journal your journey. Write down your experience, struggles, and questions so that when you gather with other disciples, you can accurately explain your battles, and articulate your lessons.

Get Fit

1 Thessalonians 5:23-24 The Message (MSG) — May God himself, the God who makes everything holy and whole, make you holy and whole, put you together—spirit, soul, and body—and keep you fit for the coming of our Master, Jesus Christ. The One who called you is completely dependable. If He said it, He'll do it!

1 Corinthians 6:19 (NIV) — Your body is the temple of the Holy Spirit, who lives in you and was given to you by God. You do not belong to yourself for God bought you with a high price. So you must honor God with your body.

Romans 12:1 (NIV) — Offer your bodies as living sacrifices, holy and pleasing to God—this is your spiritual act of worship.

1 Corinthians 10:13 (MSG) — But remember this—the wrong desires that come into your life aren't anything new and different. Many others have faced exactly the same problems before you. And no temptation is irresistible. You can trust God to keep the temptation from becoming so strong that you can't stand up against it, for he has promised this and will do what He says. He will show you how to escape temptation's power so that you can bear up patiently against it.

Full Attention

Matthew 6:34 The Message (MSG) — Give your entire attention to what God is doing right now, and don't get worked up about what may or may not happen tomorrow. God will help you deal with whatever hard things come up when the time comes.

Fill Up

Psalm 81:10 (NIV) — I am the LORD, your God, who brought you up out of the land of Egypt. Open your mouth wide, and I will fill it.

Ephesians 3:17-19 (NIV) — that Christ may dwell in your hearts through faith—that you, being rooted and grounded in love, may have strength to comprehend with all the saints what is the breadth and length and height and depth, and to know the love of Christ that surpasses knowledge, that you may be filled with all the fullness of God.

Rom. 15:13 (NIV) — May the God of hope fill you with all joy and peace in believing, so that by the power of the Holy Spirit you may abound in hope.

Ezra 8:23 (ESV) — So we fasted and implored our God for this, and he listened to our entreaty.

Esther 4:16 (ESV) — Go, gather all the Jews to be found in Susa, and hold a fast on my behalf, and do not eat or drink for three days, night or day. I and my young women will also fast as you do. Then I will go to the king, though it is against the law, and if I perish, I perish.

Reminders for the Week:

* Maintain a Consecrated Life.

Choose an area that you are aware needs more discipline and set goals to abstain, or limit in the form of fasting.

2 Samuel 12:16-22 (ESV) — David, therefore, sought God on behalf of the child. And David fasted and went in and lay all night on the ground. And the elders of his house stood beside him, to raise him from the ground, but he would not, nor did he eat food with them. On the seventh day, the child died. And the servants of David were afraid to tell him that the child was dead, for they said, "Behold, while the child was yet alive, we spoke to him, and he did not listen to us. How then can we say to him the child is dead? He may do himself some harm." But when David saw that his servants were whispering together, David understood that the child was dead. And David said to his servants, "Is the child dead?" They said, "He is dead." Then David arose from the earth and washed and anointed himself and changed his clothes. And he went into the house of the Lord and worshiped. He then went to his own house. And when he asked, they set food before him, and he ate..."

Ezra 3:5 (KJV) — ...and afterward there was a continual burnt offering, also for the new moons and for all the fixed festivals of the LORD that were consecrated, and from everyone who offered a freewill offering to the LORD.

* Remain Alert at all Times.

1 Peter 5: 8-11 (MSG) — Keep a cool head. Stay alert. The Devil is poised to pounce, and would like nothing better

than to catch you napping. Keep your guard up. You're not the only ones plunged into these hard times. It's the same with Christians all over the world. So keep a firm grip on the faith. The suffering won't last forever. It won't be long before this generous God who has great plans for us in Christ—eternal and glorious plans they are!—will have you put together and on your feet for good.

* Practice Testing the Spirits.

1 John 4 (ESV) — And by this we know that he abides in us, by the Spirit which he has given us. Beloved, do not believe every spirit, but test the spirits to see whether they are of God; for many false prophets have gone out into the world. By this, you know the Spirit of God: every spirit which confesses that Jesus Christ has come in the flesh is of God, and every spirit which does not confess Jesus is not of God. This is the spirit of antichrist, of which you heard that it was coming, and now it is in the world already. Little children, you are of God, and have overcome them; for he who is in you is greater that he who is in the world. They are of the world, therefore what they say is of the world, and the world listens to them. We are of God. Whoever knows God listens to us, and he who is not of God does not listen to us. By this, we know the spirit of truth and the spirit of error.

Notes

Notes

Notes

Notes

~ Week Four ~

DEFENSIVE FIGHTING TECHNIQUES

This week, God will reveal the tactics of the enemy and effective weaponry to defeat him. The focus is on developing your combat skills, with special emphasis on scriptural weaponry and physical fitness training. You'll learn how to identify, track, target, and engage targets with a rifle. It's all about marksmanship. This time is also spent honing your self-discipline and teamwork.

Your daily sessions should always start with prayer, meditation, and listening to the voice of God. You are more equipped than you can even imagine, learning and using defensive fighting tactics. Exercise your faith in God because 2 Thessalonians 3:3 declares that, *"the Lord is faithful, who will establish you and guard you from the evil one."* Continue to be mindful of your dietary intake and putting your ungodly desires under subjection. 1 Corinthians 9:27 (KJV) states,

But I keep under my body, and bring it into subjection: lest that by any means, when I have preached to others, I myself should be a castaway.

Let's Pray

Lord, I no longer want to walk around as an unproductive Christian. Lord, I commit myself to you wholehearted withholding nothing. Jesus fill me up with your Spirit, so I can withstand the strategies of the enemy. Amen.

As you are learning and implementing defensive fighting techniques and even biblical lifesaving skills, you may experience some interference from the enemy. The Prophet in Isaiah 59:19 declares, *So shall they fear the name of the Lord from the west, and his Glory from the rising of the sun. When the enemy shall come in like a flood, the Spirit of the Lord shall lift up a standard against him.* Again, know what to do while under enemy fire and have the knowledge you need to save your life and those of your fellow believers. The essential part of this session is communicating with God and knowing the VOICE of God.

Follow the Word of God

Philippians 4:9 — Whatever you have learned or received or heard from me, or seen in me—put it into practice. And the God of peace will be with you.

Live to Serve

1 Peter 4 (MSG) 7-11 — Everything in the world is about to be wrapped up, so take nothing for granted. Stay wide-awake in prayer. Most of all, love each other as if your life depended on it. Love makes up for practically anything. Be quick to give a meal to the hungry, a bed to the homeless— cheerfully. Be generous with the different things God gave

you, passing them around so all get in on it: if words, let it be God's Words; if help, let it be God's hearty help. That way, God's bright presence will be evident in everything through Jesus, and he'll get all the credit as the One mighty in everything—encores to the end of time. Oh, yes!

Galatians 6:10 (MSG) — So let's not allow ourselves to get fatigued doing good. At the right time, we will harvest a good crop if we don't give up, or quit. Right now, therefore, every time we get the chance, let us work for the benefit of all, starting with the people closest to us in the community of faith.

Matthew 28:19-20 — "Therefore go and make disciples of all nations, baptizing them in the name of the Father and of the Son and of the Holy Spirit, and teaching them to obey everything I have commanded you. And surely I am with you always, to the very end of the age." Jesus commands us to go out in the world.

Pray Intentionally

Outside of your daily worship and prayer, set aside time for an intentional prayer that is centered on the Word of God and His plan for you and other disciples.

Colossians 4:2 — Devote yourselves to prayer, being watchful and thankful.

Matthew 6:7 — "But when ye pray, use not vain repetitions, as the heathen do: for they think that they shall be heard for their much speaking." When you go to God, reverence Him and acknowledge who He is. Your daily struggles or goal can be included in this time of personal communication.

Know the Will and Word of God.

1 John 5:14-15 (KJV) — And this is the confidence that we have in him, that, if we ask anything according to his will, he heareth us.

Daniel 6:18 (ESV) — Then the king went to his palace and spent the night fasting; no diversions were brought to him, and sleep fled from him.

No Pain, No Gain

Those who suffer with Christ will reign with Christ.

1 Peter 3:14-18 The Message (MSG) — If with heart and soul you're doing good, do you think you can be stopped? Even if you suffer for it, you're still better off. Don't give the opposition a second thought. Through thick and thin, keep your hearts at attention, in adoration before Christ, your Master. Be ready to speak up and tell anyone who asks why you're living the way you are, and always with the utmost courtesy. Keep a clear conscience before God so that when people throw mud at you, none of it will stick. They'll end up realizing that they're the ones who need a bath. It's better to suffer for doing good, if that's what God wants, than to be punished for doing bad. That's what Christ did definitively: he suffered because of others' sins, the Righteous One for the unrighteous ones. He went through it all—was put to death and then made alive—to bring us to God.

Learn How to Breathe

Take time to refresh yourself. You cannot be an effective soldier if you do not relax and do self-care. John the Baptist records Jesus saying in Mathew 11: 28-30, "Are you tired? Worn out? Burned out on religion? Come to me. Get away with me, and you'll recover your life. I'll show you how to take a real rest. Walk with me and work with me—watch how I do it. Learn the unforced rhythms of grace. I won't lay anything heavy or ill-fitting on you. Keep company with me, and you'll learn to live freely and lightly."

Colossians 3:15 — And let the peace of Christ rule in your hearts, to which indeed you were called in one body. And be thankful.

Job 33:4 — The Spirit of God has made me, and the breath of the Almighty gives me life.

Ezekiel 37:5 — Thus says the Lord God to these bones: Behold, I will cause breath to enter you, and you shall live.

Reminders for the Week:

* Create a List of Daily Faith Scriptures

At the top of a piece of paper, write the word **Faith**. Search the Scriptures on faith and write them down; add to this list often. Recite these scriptures and commit them to your memory. There will be a time as you begin warfare that you will need to refer to this list. John 14:26 reminds us, *"But the Comforter, which is the Holy Ghost, whom the Father will send in my name, He shall teach you all things, and bring all things to your remembrance, whatsoever I have said unto you."* If you feel comfortable, do something with other words like **endurance** and **love**.

* Be Patient with Yourself, Ministry, and Other People

Romans 8:1 (AMP) — Therefore there is now no condemnation [no guilty verdict, no punishment] for those who are in Christ Jesus [who believe in Him as personal Lord and Savior]."

Ecclesiastes 9:11(KJV) — I returned, and saw under the sun, that the race is not to the swift, nor the battle to the strong, neither yet bread to the wise, nor yet riches to men of understanding, nor yet favour to men of skill; but time and chance happened to them all.

Isaiah 40:31 (KJV) — But they that wait upon the Lord shall renew their strength; they shall mount up with wings as eagles; they shall run, and not be weary, and they shall walk, and not faint.

* Practice Self-control in Talking, Emotions, and Eating

James 1: 19 (KJV) — My dear brothers and sisters, take note of this: Everyone should be quick to listen, slow to speak and slow to become angry.

1 Corinthians 9:27 (ESV) — But I discipline my body and keep it under control, lest after preaching to others I myself should be disqualified.

Proverbs 23:20-21 (ESV) — Be not among drunkards or among gluttonous eaters of meat for the drunkard and the glutton will come to poverty, and slumber will clothe them with rags.

Isaiah 58:6 (ESV) — Is not this the fast that I choose: to lose the bonds of wickedness, to undo the straps of the yoke, to let the oppressed go free, and to break every yoke?

Notes

Notes

Notes

Notes

~ Week Five ~

STRATEGIES SESSION

This week, God is allowing you to practice the weapons of warfare. Learning the importance of corporate prayer, evangelizing, fasting, and tithing is the primary focus of this strategies session.

"When you go out to battle against your enemies and see horses and chariots and people more numerous than you, do not be afraid of them; for the LORD your God, who brought you up from the land of Egypt, is with you" (Deuteronomy 20:1-4).

Your daily sessions should always start with prayer, meditation, and listening for the voice of God. It is so important that you have a healthy balance in your life. Reminding yourself that your ultimate goal as a disciple of the Trinity—Jesus Christ the Son, God the Father and the Holy Spirit the Comforter—is to accept what 1 Peter 2:9 says, *"You are a chosen people, a royal priesthood, a holy nation, God's special possession, that you may declare the praises of him who called you out of darkness into his wonderful light."* You are the heir of the Kingdom of God.

Let's Pray

Lord God, I make this commitment to myself and all others whom you have chosen me to impact. Lord, I know your Word states, the harvest is plenteous but laborers are few. God, I open myself to you, so you can create in me a clean heart and renew a right spirit in me. Amen.

This week will be the most rewarding week because skills you have learned will be applied to your everyday life. It's time to use what you have learned. The Word, prayer and goal-setting life that you have been developing alone—it is time to share with the brethren. *"You are the light of the world. A town built on a hill cannot be hidden."* (Matthew 5:14). He called you to this through our gospel, that you might share in the glory of our Lord Jesus Christ (2 Thessalonians 2:14). Paul proclaims in Romans 1:16, *For I am not ashamed of the gospel, because it is the power of God that brings salvation to everyone who believes: first to the Jew, then to the Gentile.*

We will now focus on three Strategies: Evangelizing (the Word), Interceding (prayer and fasting), and Praise & Worship.

Evangelizing

Evangelism does not have to be a scary or foreign concept. Keeping it as simple as possible is the best practice. 1 Peter 3:15 says, *But in your hearts honor Christ the Lord as holy, always being prepared to make a defense to anyone who asks you for a reason for the hope that is in you; yet do it with gentleness and respect.*

* Stay on Target.

You are now an ambassador or representative of God, Jesus Christ, to those who may have never been offered the chance for a personal relationship with Christ and to those that have. 2 Timothy 2:25 states, *Do your best to present yourself to God as one approved, a worker who has no need to be ashamed, rightly handling the Word of Truth. Stay on target with the message that you are equipped to handle.*

Luke 4:43 (ESV) — But he said to them, "I must preach the good news of the kingdom of God to the other towns as well; for I was sent for this purpose."

2 Timothy 4:18 (ESV) — The Lord will rescue me from every evil deed and bring me safely into his heavenly kingdom. To him be the glory forever and ever. Amen.

Keep notes and be specific in the motivation and goal. Just as you've journaled in your previous sessions for your understanding and edification, prepare yourself for possible questions and needs of potential converts.

2 Timothy 2:15 (NLT) — Work hard so you can present yourself to God and receive his approval. Be a good worker, one who does not need to be ashamed and who correctly explains the word of truth.

Hebrews 11:7 (ESV) — By faith Noah, being warned by God concerning events as yet unseen, in reverent fear constructed an ark for the saving of his household. By this, he condemned the world and became an heir of the righteousness that comes by faith.

* Be Serious, but not Harsh; There is a Time and Season for Everything.

1 Peter 2:1-25 (ESV) — So put away all malice and all deceit and hypocrisy and envy and all slander. Like newborn infants, long for the pure spiritual milk, that by it you may grow up into salvation— if indeed you have tasted that the Lord is good. As you come to him, a living stone rejected by men but in the sight of God chosen and precious, you yourselves like living stones are being built up as a spiritual house, to be a holy priesthood, to offer spiritual sacrifices acceptable to God through Jesus Christ.

Galatians 5:19-21 (ESV) — Now the works of the flesh are evident: sexual immorality, impurity, sensuality, idolatry, sorcery, enmity, strife, jealousy, fits of anger, rivalries, dissensions, divisions, envy, drunkenness, orgies, and things like these. I warn you, as I warned you before, that those who do such things will not inherit the Kingdom of God.

* Learn How to Walk Away. Be Mindful that Badgering or Browbeating is the Worse.

Matthew 10:14 (NIV) — If anyone will not welcome you or listen to your words, leave that home or town and shake the dust off your feet.

1 Peter 2:1-25 — So put away all malice and all deceit and hypocrisy and envy and all slander. Like newborn infants, long for the pure spiritual milk, that by it you may grow up into salvation— if indeed you have tasted that the Lord is good. As you come to him, a living stone rejected by men but in the sight of God chosen and precious, you yourselves

like living stones are being built up as a spiritual house, to be a holy priesthood, to offer spiritual sacrifices acceptable to God through Jesus Christ…

Matthew 13:24-30 (ESV) — He put another parable before them, saying, "The kingdom of heaven may be compared to a man who sowed good seed in his field, but while his men were sleeping, his enemy came and sowed weeds among the wheat and went away. So when the plants came up and bore grain, then the weeds appeared as well. And the servants of the master of the house came and said to him, 'Master, did you not sow good seed in your field? How then does it have weeds?' He said to them, 'An enemy has done this.' So the servants said to him, 'Then do you want us to go and gather them?'"

Interceding

Intercession is a very powerful and effective weapon of warfare in the Kingdom of God. James 5:16 (KJV) says, *Confess your faults one to another, and pray one for another, that ye may be healed. The effectual fervent prayer of a righteous man availeth much.* This weapon is the most effective one because you are exposing the problem or enemy tactic, identifying the will of God, then getting in the presence of God for a supernatural breakthrough.

* Coordinate

Be purposeful in this time of fellowship. Know the reason for the prayer and what your role is in this.

Acts 14:22 — Strengthening the souls of the disciples,

encouraging them to continue in the faith, and saying that through many tribulations we must enter the kingdom of God.

Ezekiel 22:30 — And I searched for a man among them who should build up the wall and stand in the gap before Me for the land, that I should not destroy it, but I found no one.

1 Corinthians 14:16 — What then shall we say, brothers and sisters? When you come together, each of you has a hymn, or a word of instruction, a revelation, a tongue or an interpretation. Everything must be done so that the church may be built up.

* Know that God is the Author and Finisher of our Faith.

1 Corinthians 2:9 — But, as it is written, "What no eye has seen, nor ear heard, nor the heart of man imagined, what God has prepared for those who love him"

Acts 14:22 — Strengthening the souls of the disciples, encouraging them to continue in the faith, and saying that through many tribulations we must enter the kingdom of God.

Ezekiel 22:30 — And I searched for a man among them who should build up the wall and stand in the gap before Me for the land, that I should not destroy it, but I found no one.

Judges 20:26 (ESV) — Then all the people of Israel, the whole army, went up and came to Bethel and wept. They sat there before the Lord and fasted that day until evening, and offered burnt offerings and peace offerings before the Lord.

Praise and Worship

Acts 16: 25-34 (NIV) — 25 About midnight, Paul and Silas were praying and singing hymns to God, and the other prisoners were listening to them. 26 Suddenly there was such a violent earthquake that the foundations of the prison were shaken. At once all the prison doors flew open, and everyone's chains came loose. 27 The jailer woke up, and when he saw the prison doors open, he drew his sword and was about to kill himself because he thought the prisoners had escaped. 28 But Paul shouted, "Don't harm yourself! We are all here!" 29 The jailer called for lights, rushed in and fell trembling before Paul and Silas. 30 He then brought them out and asked, "Sirs, what must I do to be saved?" 31 They replied, "Believe in the Lord Jesus, and you will be saved — you and your household." 32 Then they spoke the word of the Lord to him and to all the others in his house. 33 At that hour of the night the jailer took them and washed their wounds; then immediately he and all his household were baptized. 34 The jailer brought them into his house and set a meal before them; he was filled with joy because he had come to believe in God — he and his whole household.

John 4:23 — The true worshipers will worship the Father in spirit and truth; for the Father is seeking such to worship Him. God is Spirit, and those who worship Him must worship in spirit and truth.

Revelation 4:11 — You are worthy, O Lord, to receive glory and honor and power; For You created all things, and by Your will they exist and were created.

Psalm 29:2 — Give unto the Lord the glory due to His name; worship the Lord in the beauty of holiness.

Psalm 107:14-16 — He brought them out of darkness and the shadow of death, and broke their chains in pieces. Oh, that men would give thanks to the Lord for His goodness, and for His wonderful works to the children of men! For He has broken the gates of bronze, and cut the bars of iron in two.

Reminders for the Week:

* Excellence Does Not Mean You're Flawless.

1 John 1:8-10 — If we go around bragging, "We have no sin," then we are fooling ourselves and are strangers to the truth.

Romans 3:23 — For all have sinned and fall short of the glory of God, 24 and all are justified freely by his grace through the redemption that came by Christ Jesus.

* You are an Ambassador of Christ, not God.

2 Chronicles 20:15 (KJV) — And he said, Hearken ye, all Judah, and ye inhabitants of Jerusalem, and thou king Jehoshaphat, Thus saith the Lord unto you, Be not afraid nor dismayed by reason of this great multitude; for the battle is not yours, but God's.

Proverbs 3:1-35 (ESV) — My son, do not forget my teaching, but let your heart keep my commandments, for length of days and years of life and peace they will add to you. Let not steadfast love and faithfulness forsake you; bind them around your neck; write them on the tablet of your heart. So you will find favor and good success in the sight of God and man. Trust in the Lord with all your heart, and do not lean on your own understanding....

* Repent When You Err, but do NOT GIVE UP.

Romans 7:19-25 (KJV) — 19 For the good that I would I do not: but the evil which I would not, that I do. 20 Now if I do that I would not, it is no more I that do it, but sin that dwelleth in me. 21 I find then a law, that, when I would do good, evil is present with me. 22 For I delight in the law of God after the inward man: 23 But I see another law in my members, warring against the law of my mind, and bringing me into captivity to the law of sin which is in my members. 24 O wretched man that I am! Who shall deliver me from the body of this death? 25 I thank God through Jesus Christ our Lord. So then with the mind, I myself serve the law of God; but with the flesh the law of sin.

* Surround Yourself with Good Counsel.

Proverbs 19:20-21 — Listen to advice and accept instruction, that you may gain wisdom in the future. Many are the plans in the mind of a man, but it is the purpose of the Lord that will stand.

Proverbs 28:26 (ESV) — Whoever trusts in his own mind is a fool, but he who walks in wisdom will be delivered.

1 Corinthians 15:33 (ESV) — Do not be deceived: "Bad company ruins good morals."

Notes

Notes

Notes

Notes

~ Week Six ~

FINAL EVALUATION

Confirmation of your role as Warrior in the Kingdom of God.

Your daily sessions should always start with prayer, meditation, and listening to the voice of God.

Let's Pray

Lord God, thank you for the Gift that you have entrusted me with.

Corinthians 5:17 (KJV) — Therefore if any man be in Christ, he is a new creature: old things are passed away; behold, all things become new.

You are now spiritually fit to handle the adversary! The Bible declares according to Luke 10:19, *Behold, I give unto you power to tread on serpents and scorpions, and over all the powers of the enemy: and nothing shall by any means hurt you.* During this session, the Holy Spirit should have been invited to come into this newness of life within you. The new doors of your heart are open to receive the fresh wind of the Holy Spirit.

In this session, believe in God's power, according to Acts 1:8, *But ye shall receive power, after that the Holy Ghost is come upon you: and ye shall be witness unto me both in Jerusalem, and in all Judaea, and in Samaria, and unto the uttermost part of the earth.* There is a new fight, a new rest, a new peace that surpasses all understand according to Philippians 4:7 (ESV), *"And the peace of God, which surpasses all understanding, will guard your hearts and your minds in Christ Jesus."*

A new breath of life should be consuming you because you understand the powers that be, according to Romans 8:10-12, *And if Christ be in you, the body is dead because of sin; but the Spirit is life because of righteousness, But if the Spirit of him that raised up Jesus from the dead dwell in you, he that raised up Christ from the dead shall quicken your mortal bodies by his Spirit that dwelleth in you. Therefore, brethren, we are debtors, not to the flesh, to live after the flesh.*

So now, we no longer live by the flesh because the Spirit of the living God has consumed us during these six weeks of BST, and "*God has not given us the spirit of fear; but of power, and of love, and of a sound mind,*" according to 2 Timothy 1:7.

Wherefore I put thee in remembrance that thou stir up the gift of God, which is in thee by the putting on of my hand (2 Timothy 1:6 KJV). In these sessions, God has charged you by laying hands on you with the word of God and the Apostle. Gird up yourselves with all the truths that you have learned, you are not only hearers of the word, according to James 1:22-25, "*but doers of the word, and not hearers only, deceiving yourselves. for if anyone is a hearer of the word and not a doer, he is like a man who looks intently at his natural face in the mirror. For he looks at himself and goes away and at once forgets what he was like. But the one who looks into the perfect law, the law of liberty, and perseveres, being no hearer who forgets but a doer who acts, he will be blessed in his doing.*

How many of you like what you see now? This is always a clearer view when the Spirit of God comes in and makes residence in us.

Are you ready to stand against the wiles of the devil?
Let's Go!
Orders
Walking it out
Posture
Notes on lessons learned
Follow, are you following?
Worship
Final Test
Positioned – Who are you?

Notes

Notes

Notes

Notes

ACCOMPLISHMENTS

You'll celebrate your achievement in front of other believers, you are ready, and we are listening. Nothing is stopping you now. Faith comes by hearing the Word of God. No more double-minded Christians, you shall have the things you speak.

ABOUT THE AUTHOR

Apostle Deborah Sheppard

Deborah Sheppard is the co-founder of Unveiling Word Ministries Newnan, Ga., with her husband, Apostle Wayne Sheppard. She is a loving mother of three wonderful boys, Immanuel Griggs, Darrell Griggs, and Elijah Griggs.

Apostle Deborah Sheppard Graduated from Newnan High School in 1986, she received her Master's in Cosmetology in 1993, her second Degree in Business Administration in 2005 at the American InterContinental University, and went on to receive her third Degree in Accounting/Banking in 2012 from the Rasmussen University in Ocala, FL. She is also a graduate of Leadership Coweta 2013's Coweta County Chamber of Commerce.

Apostle Deborah Sheppard's spiritual covering is Bishop Timothy O. Boone and Pastor Cynthia Boone.

Apostle Deborah Sheppard is a successful entrepreneur, the past owner of Emmanuel Hair Salon, MFC Financial Service LLC (Tax Preparation and Financial Consultancy), and The Queen Jewels & Apparel LLC. Apostle Deborah's passion is helping serve the community, she has three current projects that she oversees — Community Kidz Back to School project; Project 21; and Christmas Project, where she adopts 21 children at Christmas time. This is just to name a few. Apostle Deborah is driven to give her best in the Kingdom of God by building great relationships.

Apostle Deborah Sheppard, a soul winner for the Kingdom of God, displays it with a driven passion of Christ's Love, walks heavy in the Prophetic, and is a determined no soul-left-behind! Over 20 years of running and doing Kingdom business, being developed in the Apostolic Realm of the Spirit, Apostle Deborah challenges others to "Rethink" so God can develop Christ's character in them. Apostle declares the best is yet to come in the Kingdom of God! Her goal is to reach the world with the teaching of Jesus Christ through the HOLY SPIRIT.

Apostle Deborah now has a women ministry called "Sister 2 Sister, Real Talk #Iammysisterkeeper" with the goal of bringing healing and imparting new hope and comfort to the brokenhearted. Apostle Deborah is pressing toward the mark of the higher calling which is in Christ Jesus.

www.ingramcontent.com/pod-product-compliance
Lightning Source LLC
Chambersburg PA
CBHW071332190426
43193CB00041B/1748